The Joy of Piano

It was Signor Bartolommeo Cristofori,
the imaginative instrument maker of Florence, who
in 1709 made the first piano. He probably never envisioned
that his invention the 'piano e forte' would for centuries
be the most popular and widely used of all musical
instruments. And, this 'wonderous box', as
Oliver Wendell Holmes once called it,
continues to grow in popularity. Today, more people
study piano for sheer pleasure than at any time in history.

THE JOY OF PIANO was compiled and arranged by Denes Agay.
It contains a colorful and well-balanced storehouse
of easy-to-play piano melodies. The player will
enjoy familiar themes by the masters,
folk tunes, favorite standard songs and popular
melodies of today. The variety is pleasing and educational.
Mr. Agay's musical arrangements are simple and
full sounding. Pianists of all ages will
appreciate the musical quality that has
made his work so widely known.

US International Standard Book Number: 0.8256.8002.6
UK International Standard Book Number: 0.7119.0131.7

Exclusive Distributors:
Music Sales Corporation
225 Park Avenue South, New York, NY 10003 USA
Music Sales Limited
8/9 Frith Street, London W1V 5TZ England
Music Sales Pty. Limited
120 Rothschild Street, Rosebery, Sydney, NSW 2018, Australia

Printed in the United States of America by
Vicks Lithograph and Printing Corporation

Contents

Symphony No. 7
(Theme from 2nd Movement)

Ludwig van Beethoven

Allegretto

Symphony No.1
(Theme - Finale)

Johannes Brahms

Moderate, steady motion

Lullaby

Johannes Brahms

Caprice No. 24

Niccolo Paganini

Bright

New World Symphony

(Theme from 2nd Movement)

Anton Dvorak

Slowly

Piano Concerto No.3
(Theme from 1st Movement)

Ludwig van Beethoven

Piano Concerto
(Theme)

Edvard Grieg

Moderately fast

Pomp and Circumstance

Edward Elgar

Broadly and solemnly

Nocturne

Moderately

Frederic Chopin

Tempo indication in the original is $\frac{12}{8}$

Saint Anthony Chorale

Joseph Haydn

Moderate walking tempo

Sheep May Safely Graze

(Theme from the "Birthday Cantata")

Johann Sebastian Bach

Gently moving

Unfinished Symphony
(Theme)

Franz Schubert

Moderately

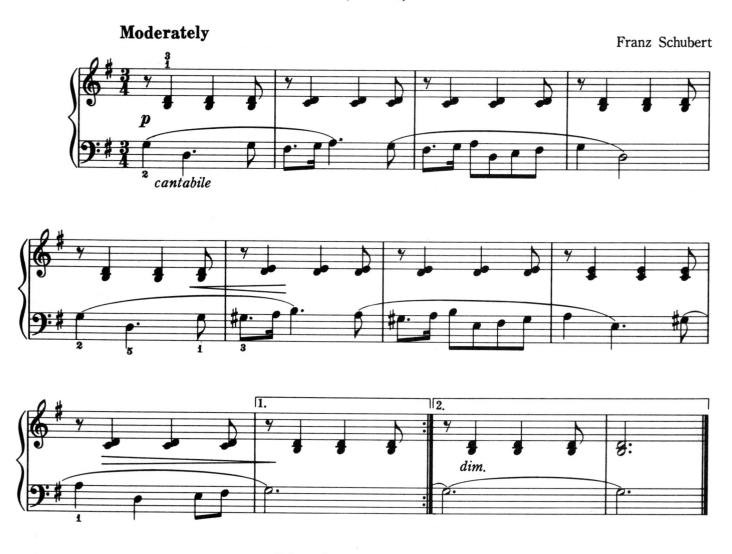

To A Wild Rose

Edward MacDowell

With simple tenderness

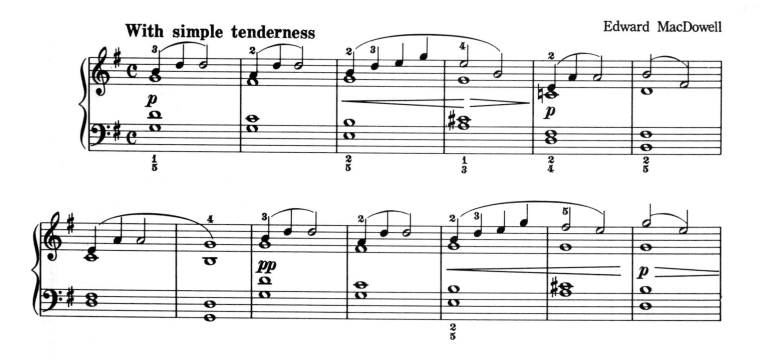

Piano Concerto No. 1
(Theme from 1st Movement)

Peter I. Tchaikovsky

Symphony No.5
(Theme from 2nd Movement)

Peter I. Tchaikovsky

Slowly

Clair de Lune

Slowly, with expression

Claude Debussy

Slavonic Dance No. 10

Anton Dvorak

Freely moving

Polovetzian Dance

Alexander Borodin

Comedians' Galop

Dmitri Kabalevsky

Hungarian Dance No. 4

Johannes Brahms

D.C. al Fine

Gavotte
（from Violin Sonata No. 6）

Johann Sebastian Bach

Graceful walking tempo

Farandole
(from L'Arlesienne Suite No. 2)

Georges Bizet

Mattinata

Ruggiero Leoncavallo

Freely moving

Waltzes by Strauss
(Themes)

Moderately

"The Emperor Waltz"

Johann Strauss

"Wine, Women, and Song"

La Ci Darem La Mano
(Duet from "Don Giovanni")

Wolfgang A. Mozart

Comfortable walking tempo

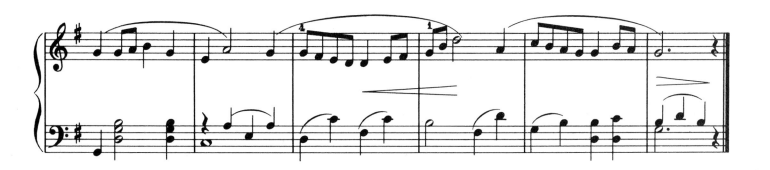

Toreador Song

(from "Carmen")

Georges Bizet

Moderately, with vigor

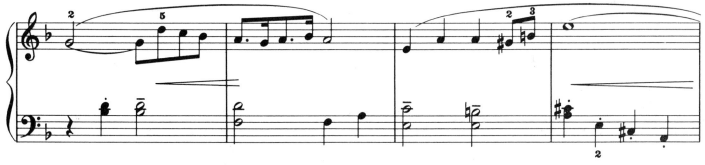

Madame Butterfly
(Themes)

Giacomo Puccini

Broadly

Very slow ("Un bel di")

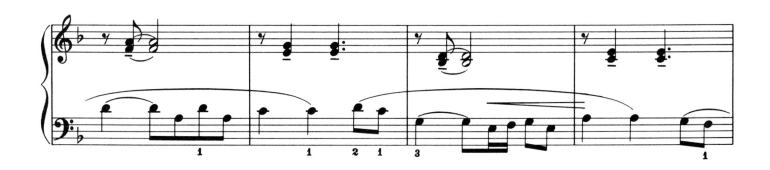

My Heart At Thy Sweet Voice
（from "Samson and Delilah"）

Moderately slow

Camille Saint-Saëns

The Bell Song
(from "Lakmé")

Leo Delibes

Tit - Willow
(from "The Mikado")

William S. Gilbert

Arthur Sullivan

Moderately, with warmth

On a tree by the riv-er a lit-tle tom-tit Sang_ "Wil-low, tit-wil-low, tit-wil-low"_____ And I said to him "Dick-y-bird, why do you sit" Sing-ing "Wil-low, tit-wil-low, tit-wil-low?"_____ "Is it weak-ness of in-tel-lect, bird-ie?" I cried, "Or a rath-er tough worm in your lit-tle in-side?" With a shake of his poor lit-tle head, he re-plied, "Oh, wil-low, tit-wil-low, tit-wil-low!"_____

Pirate Chorus
(from "The Pirates Of Penzance")

William S. Gilbert

Moderate march tempo

Arthur Sullivan

mp With cat-like tread Up - on our prey we steal, In si - lence dread Our cau-tious way we feel!

No sound at all, We nev-er speak a word; A fly's foot-fall Would be dis-tinct - ly heard!

f Come, friends, who plow the sea, Truce to nav-i - ga - tion, Take an-oth-er sta - tion;

Let's var - y pi - ra - cee, With a lit-tle bur-gla - ree!

The Merry Widow Waltz

Franz Lehár

Moderate waltz tempo

Toyland
(from "Babes In Toyland")

Glen MacDonough

Victor Herbert

Glow Worm

Lila Cayley Robinson

Paul Lincke

Beautiful Dreamer

Stephen Foster

Mighty Lak' A Rose

Ethelbert Nevin

When The Saints Come Marchin' In

Spirited walking tempo

Traditional

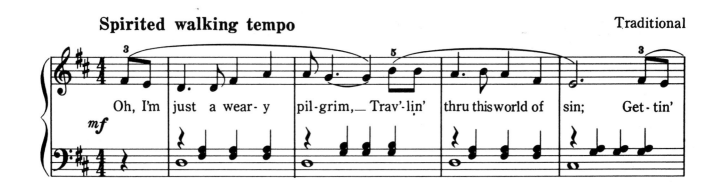

Oh, I'm just a wear-y pil-grim,— Trav'-lin' thru this world of sin; Get-tin'

read-y for the day ——— When the saints come march-in' in.——— Oh, when the

saints——— come march-in' in, When the saints come march-in' in, Lord, I

want to be in that num-ber,——— When the saints come march-in' in.

Sweet Betsy From Pike

Folk Song

Moderately bright

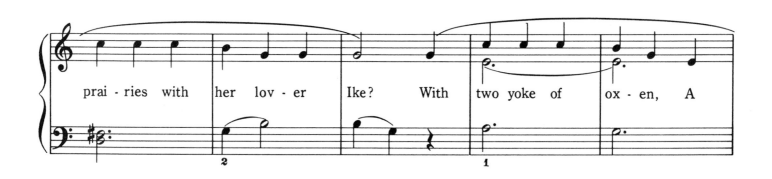

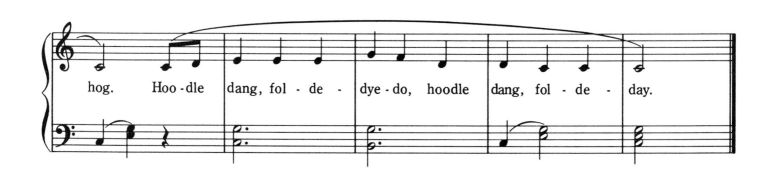

When I Was Single

Lively and robust

Folk Song

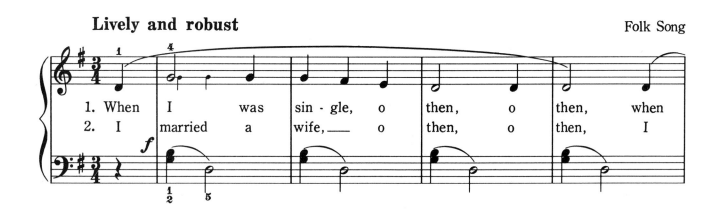

1. When I was sin - gle, o then, o then, when
2. I married a wife, — o then, o then, I

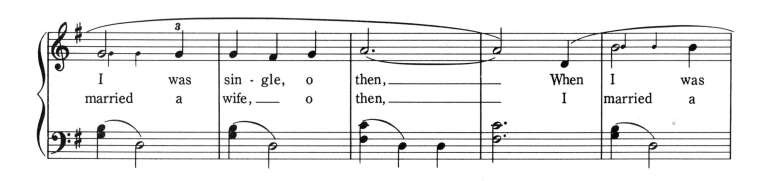

I was sin - gle, o then, — When I was
married a wife, — o then, — I married a

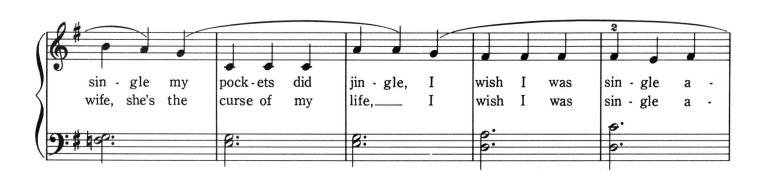

sin - gle my pock - ets did jin - gle, I wish I was sin - gle a -
wife, she's the curse of my life, — I wish I was sin - gle a -

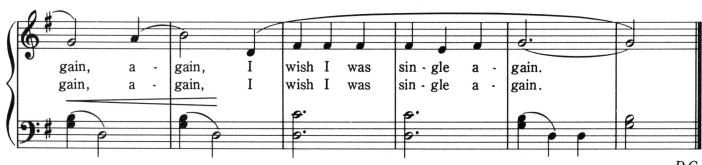

gain, a - gain, I wish I was sin - gle a - gain.
gain, a - gain, I wish I was sin - gle a - gain.

D.C.

Li'l Liza Jane

Folk Song

Bright

I know a gal that I a - dore, Li'l Li - za Jane,

'Way down south in Bal - ti - more, Li'l Li - za Jane.

Oh, E - li - za, Li'l Li - za Jane,

Oh, E - li - za, Li'l Li - za Jane!

Red River Valley

Cowboy Song

Lively

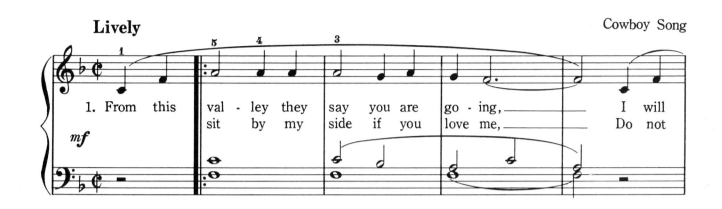

1. From this valley they say you are go - ing, _____ I will
   sit by my side if you love me, _____ Do not

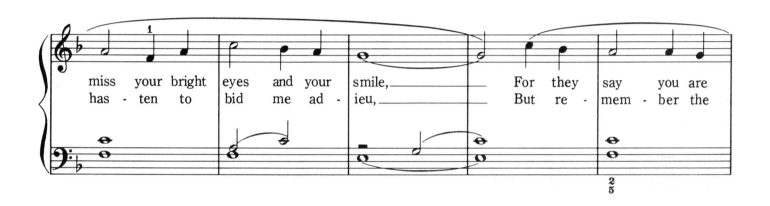

miss your bright eyes and your smile, _____ For they say you are
has - ten to bid me ad - ieu, _____ But re - mem - ber the

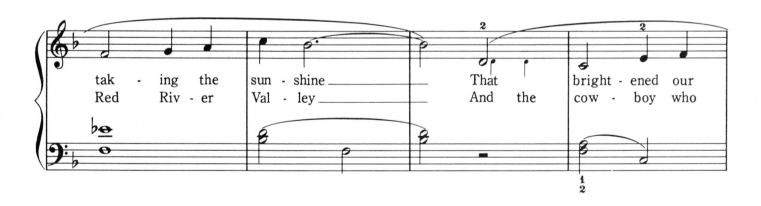

tak - ing the sun - shine _____ That bright - ened our
Red Riv - er Val - ley _____ And the cow - boy who

path - way a - while. _____ 2. Come and
loved you so true.

Polly Wolly Doodle

Traditional

Lively

Oh I went down South for to see my Sal, sing-ing Pol-ly Wol-ly Doo-dle all the

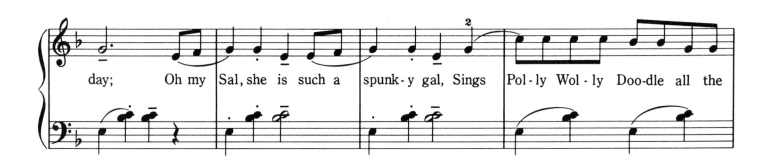

day; Oh my Sal, she is such a spunk-y gal, Sings Pol-ly Wol-ly Doo-dle all the

day. *f* Fare thee well, Fare thee well, Fare thee well my fair-y fay, For I'm

gwine to Lou-si-an-na, my gui-tar and her "pi-an-a," Sing-ing Pol-ly Wol-ly Doo-dle all the day.

The Yellow Rose Of Texas

Traditional

Bright

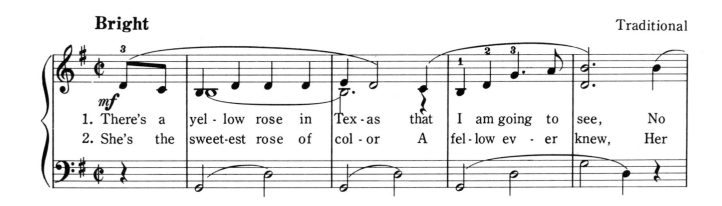

1. There's a yel-low rose in Tex-as that I am going to see, No oth-er fel-low knows her, No fel-low on-ly me, She cried so when I left her, It like to break my heart, And if I ev-er find her We nev-er more will part.

2. She's the sweet-est rose of col-or A fel-low ev-er knew, Her eyes are bright as di'-monds, They spark-le like the dew, You may talk a-bout your dear-est May, And sing of Ro-sa Lee, But the yel-low rose of Tex-as beats the belles of Ten-nes-see.

D.C.

Down By The Riverside

(I Ain't Gonna Study War No More)

Moderately with spirit

Folk Song

The Blue Tail Fly

Folk Song

Freely

When I was young I used to wait On my mas-ter and hand him his plate, And

Lively

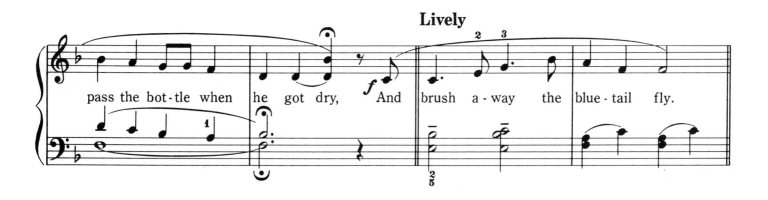

pass the bot-tle when he got dry, And brush a-way the blue-tail fly.

Jim-my crack corn and I don't care, Jim-my crack corn and I don't care,

Jim-my crack corn and I don't care, My mas-ter's gone a-way!

I've Been Workin' On The Railroad

Traditional

Happy walking tempo

I've been work-in' on the rail - road All the live - long day,

I've been work-in' on the rail - road, Just to pass the time a - way.

Don't you hear the whis - tle blow - in', Rise up so ear - ly in the morn?

Don't you hear the cap - tain call - in' "Din - ah, blow your horn!"?

Down In The Valley

Moderately

Folk Song

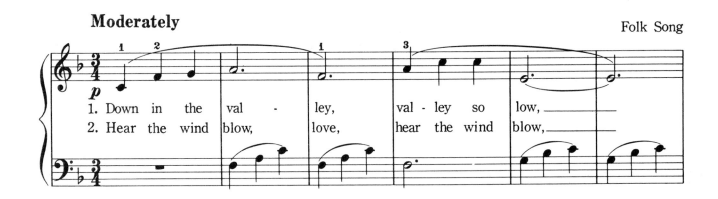

1. Down in the val - ley, val - ley so low,
2. Hear the wind blow, love, hear the wind blow,

Hang your head o - ver, hear the wind blow.
Hang your head o - ver, hear the wind blow.

Aunt Rhody Boogie

Traditional
adapted by Denes Agay

Lively boogie tempo

Fascination

Filippo D. Marchetti

Slow waltz

Amoureuse
（Valse　Continentale）

Slow waltz

Rudolphe Berger

Moscow Nights

V. Soloviev-Sedoy

The Whistler And His Dog

Moderate walking tempo

Arthur Pryor

D.C. al Fine

The Kerry Dance

James L. Molloy

Bright

O the days of the Ker-ry danc-ing, O the ring of the pi-per's tune! O for one of those hours of glad-ness, Gone a-las like our youth, too soon.

When the boys be-gan to gath-er in the glen, of a sum-mer night,

And the Ker-ry pi-per's tun-ing made us long—with wild de-light;

O to think of it, O to dream of it, Fills my heart with tears!

D.S. al Fine

Loch Lomond

Walking tempo

Scotch Air

Parade Of The Tin Soldiers

Leon Jessel

Lively and gracefully

D.C. al Fine

Down South

Bright, strutting tempo

W. H. Myddleton

Chicken Reel

Traditional Fiddle Tune

When You Were Sweet Sixteen

James Thornton

Sweet Adeline

Richard H. Gerard

Moderately slow

Harry Armstrong

In My Merry Oldsmobile

Vincent Bryant

Gus Edwards

The Band Played On

John F. Palmer

Charles B. Ward

Daisy Bell
(Bicycle Built For Two)

Harry Dacre

Bright waltz tempo

Dai - sy, Dai - sy, Give me your an - swer, do; I'm half cra - zy All for the love of you. It won't be a styl - ish mar - riage, I can't af - ford a car - riage, but you'd look sweet up - on a seat Of a bi - cy - cle built for two.

My Gal Sal

Paul Dresser

Moderately

They called her fri-vo-lous Sal, A pe-cu-liar sort of a gal, With a heart that was mel-low, An all 'round good fel-low, Was my old pal. Your trou-bles, sor-rows and care, She was al-ways will-ing to share. A wild sort of dev-il, But dead on the lev-el, Was my gal Sal.

Give My Regards To Broadway

George M. Cohan

Wait 'Till The Sun Shines, Nellie

Andrew B. Sterling

Harry von Tilzer

I Love You Truly

Carrie Jacobs-Bond

Rather slow

p
1. I love you tru - ly, tru - ly dear,
2. Ah! love, 'tis some - thing to feel your kind hand,

Life with its sor - row, life with its tear,
Ah! yes, 'tis some - thing by your side to stand;

Fades in - to dreams when I feel you are near,
Gone is the sor - row, gone doubt and fear,

rit.

For I love you tru - ly, tru - ly, dear. *p*

Dear Old Girl

Richard Henry Buck

Theodore F. Morse

Hello! Ma Baby

Howard and Emerson

Lively ragtime

When Johnny Comes Marching Home

Lively march tempo

Traditional

America, The Beautiful

Katherine L. Bates

Samuel A. Ward

Moderately

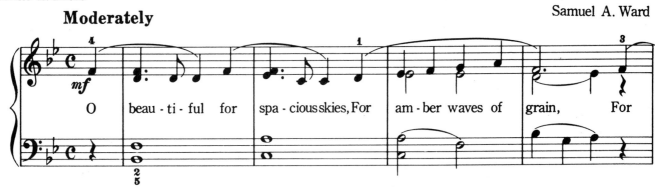

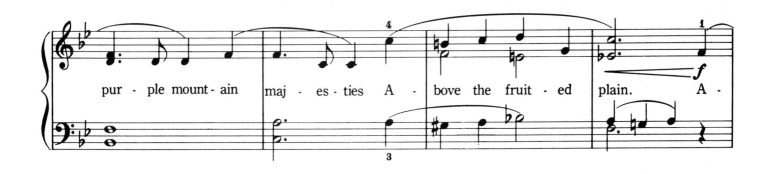

O beau-ti-ful for spa-cious skies, For am-ber waves of grain, For

pur-ple mount-ain maj-es-ties A-bove the fruit-ed plain. A-

mer-i-ca! A-mer-i-ca! God shed His grace on thee, And

crown thy good with broth-er-hood From sea to shin-ing sea!

Printing No 6, 7, 8, 9